Phu Quoc I
20 Milestone

CW00687897

Phu Quoc Ridgeback Memorable Moments. Includes Milestones for Memories, Gifts, Socialization & Training

Volume 1

Todays Doggy

Copyright © 2019

Dedicated To All of You Wonderful Owners and Fans

Introduction

Welcome to the Original Doggy Milestone Series™ where you are encouraged to create those special moments with your dog. We have composed the milestones in a way that challenges you to set the stage before taking your photos.

Use props and make it fun - be creative in setting up your photos. Get family and friends involved - take it out with you - use it in different places and settings - have a play with it and most importantly, have a good time!

You can either hold the desired milestone spread open yourself - or have somebody hold it open as you take the snap.

If you would like to have the selected milestone book spread open and standing independently in your photos, you can use one or two large 'foldback' clips to hold the spread open.

Good luck and enjoy your photo fun.

I Love
My
Family...

...And My Family Loves Me

At The
Beach!

Having a

Wave

of a

Time

NIGHT OUT

With My Doggy Pals

IT'S...

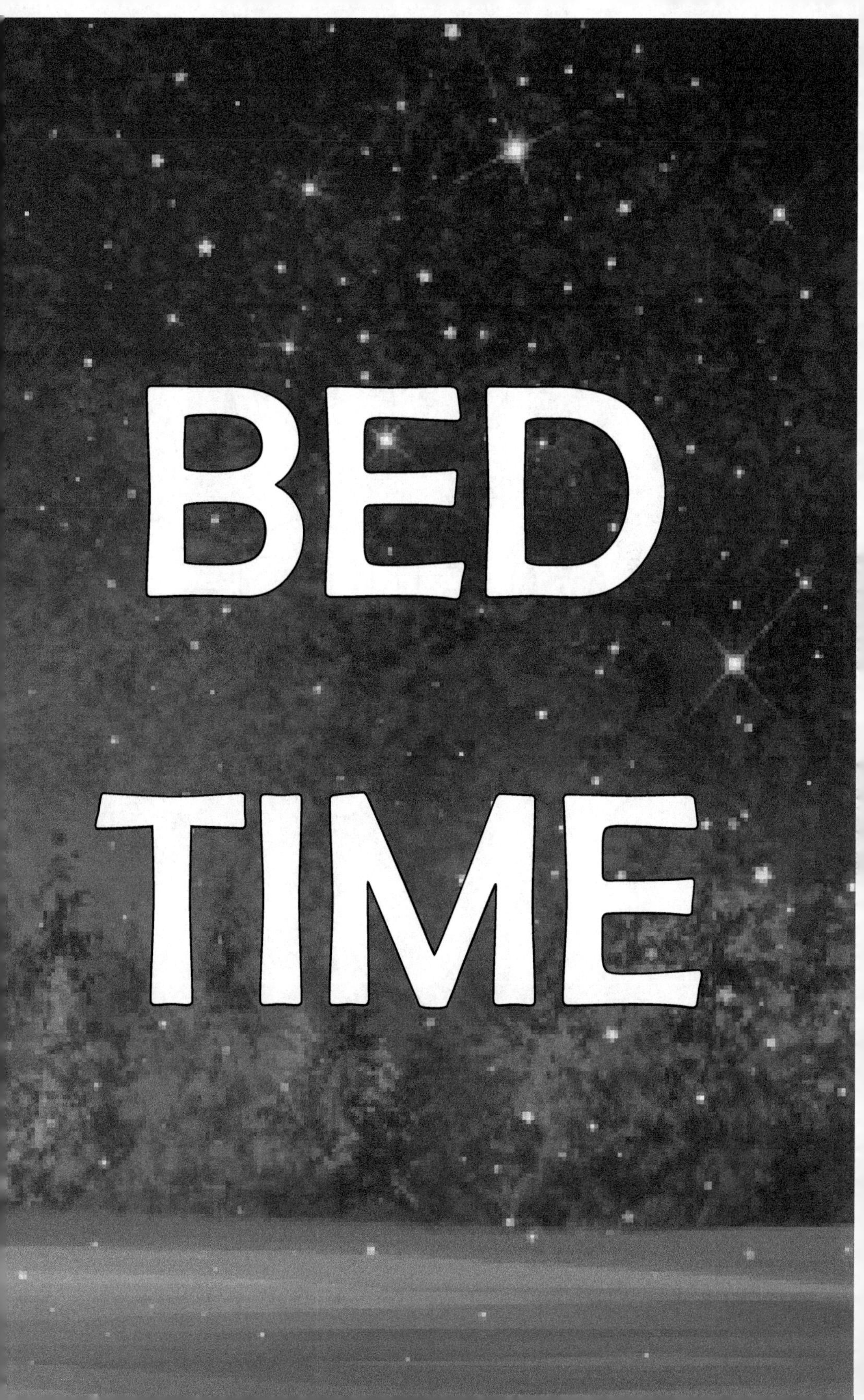
BED
TIME

I DIDN'T KNOW WHICH STICK YOU THREW

SO I BOUGHT BACK ALL OF THEM

They Say Diamonds Are a Girl's Best Friend

I Disagree! I'm The Only "Best Friend" Here!

I'm Going To Start Eating Healthy...

Next
Week!

DO
NOT
DISTURB

PLAYING

IN THE

LEAVES

I Need

a

HUGe

Amount of Treats

Say

ello

OFF
To
The
VET??

CATCH ME IF YOU CAN!

KEEP

CALM

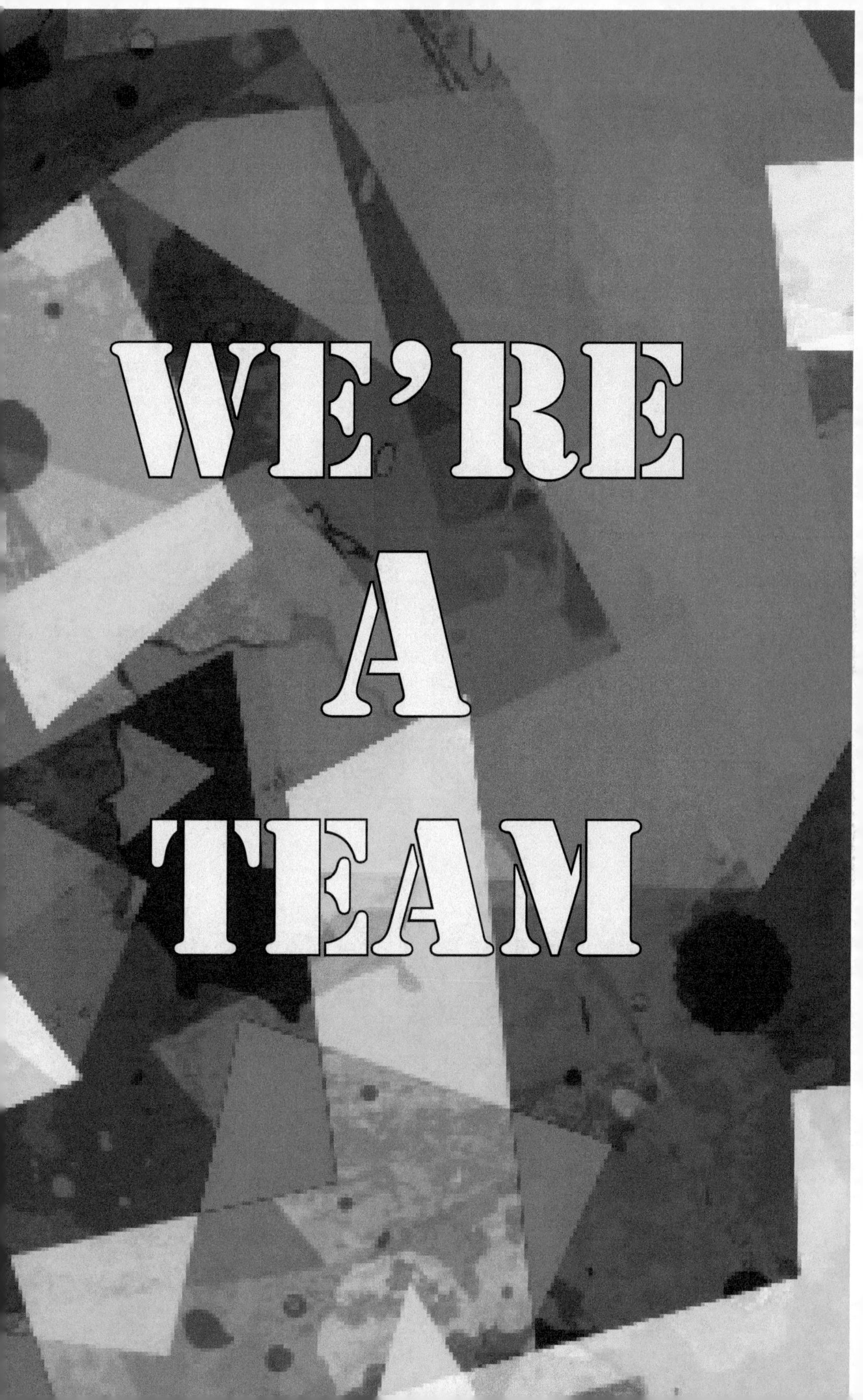
WE'RE
A
TEAM

NASA Wants To Hire Me

Because I'm a STAR!

OOPS!
I
Buried
Your
Stuff

...But I

Forgot

Where

I'm a Super Hero

My Real Name Is SUPER POOCH

Very
Incredible
Pup

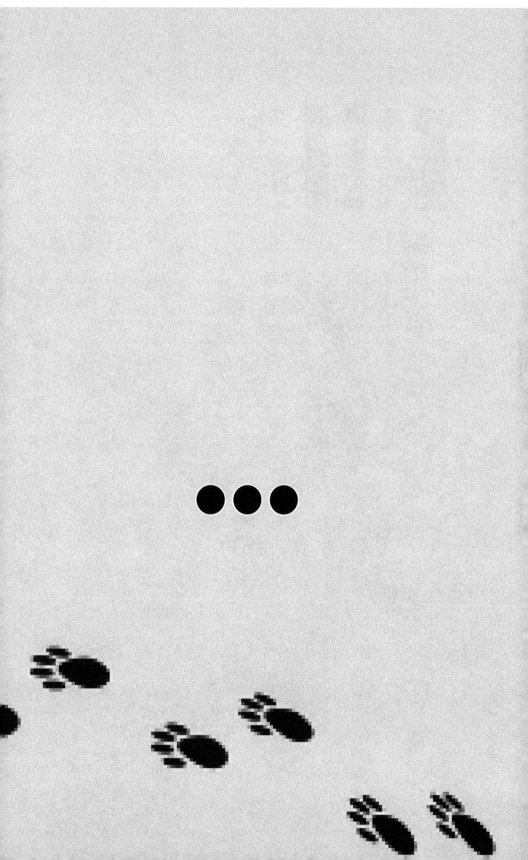

I'll Just Be Over Here...

Looking
Fabulous

PLEASE

PLEASE

PRETTY PLEEEASE

CAN I KEEP IT?

I'm
On a
SEAFOOD
Diet

CPSIA information can be obtained
at www.ICGtesting.com
Printed in the USA
LVHW081717200819
628164LV00011BA/1892/P

9 781395 331016